I0528391

CARL M. MOORE

TAKE the WORLD by STORM

TAKE THE WORLD BY STORM
Copyright © 2024 **Carl M. Moore**

ISBN (Paperback): 978-1-958475-57-7
ISBN (Ebook): 978-1-958475-58-4

All rights reserved. No part of this book may be used or reproduced by any means, graphic, electronic, or mechanical, including photocopying, recording, taping or by information storage and retrieval system without the written permission of the author except in the case of brief quotations embodied in critical articles and reviews.

Because of the dynamic nature of the Internet, any web addresses or links contained in this book may have changed since publication and may no longer be valid. The views expressed in the work are solely those of the author and do not necessarily reflect the views of the publisher, and the publisher hereby disclaims any responsibility for them.

Printed in the United States of America.

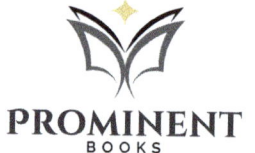

PROMINENT
BOOKS

5830 E 2nd St, Ste 7000 #9983
Casper, WY 82609
USA

ACKNOWLEDGMENT

I WOULD LIKE to acknowledge and thank Ms. Mary Mooney, Coordinator of the Interpreter Training Program at El Paso Community College (ECC) in El Paso, TX, who gave me this mug in between 1986 and 1988, which it stated, "You're an exceptional man…. There's never been anyone with your personality, ability, and unique way of seeing things. There's never been a man like you before, and there won't be again…. So go ahead! Take the world by storm! You've got what it takes!"

Linda Lee Elrod

DEDICATION

THIS BOOK IS dedicated to my parents, Rev. Carl A. Moore and Mrs. Naomi Moore, who taught me how to overcome the challenges I encountered in my life, in my disability, in my education, in my home environment, and in my work.

CONTENTS

FOREWORD

Take the World by Storm is a fitting title for the author, Carl Moore's fourth book. As Carl's friend and professional colleague, it is evident to me that he is quickly becoming a prolific author. Through his biblical stories and lessons, he also shares stories about his own life. An example of his sharing stories about his life can be found in chapter 7 of his book, *Take the World by Storm.* Chapter 7 describes what inspired him to become a minister. For interested readers, more insight about Carl's life and upbringing can be found in his third book titled, *Brotherly Love.*

Glenn B. Anderson, Ph.D.
Little Rock, AR

*   *   *

It is my pleasure to present this timely work and her author to you, the reader. At the time of this writing, As the Ministering Evangelist for the Cedar Crest Church of Christ in Dallas, Tx, I have had the pleaser of working along with brother Carl Moore for 3 and half years. In that time, he has proven himself to be a very faithful servant of God and family man. His love for Christ, God's people and family have been a model for others, and an inspiration to me. His skill in writing and organizing, coupled with his ability to connect with and teach others has undoubtedly resulted in many surrendering their lives to Jesus over the years.

His latest literary work, *Taking the World by Storm*, is another example of giftedness as a writer and a student of The Bible. This book will prove to be an essential help to anyone to seeks to become more familiar with the fundamentals of the Christian faith, the basic elements of The Bible and principles for Christian living. Through numerous and appropriate references of scripture, the reader will be challenged to come to know God in new and deeper ways.

The reader will grow in appreciation for nature and person of God. The reader will learn from biblical insights how to better treat and relate to others in the world in a Go-pleasing way. And, perhaps most importantly, any person who has yet to embrace Christ as Lord and King will be given a clear path to relationship with Him. The reader will walk away from this reading with a clear challenge to respond to t call of God to take the world by storm.

Jonathan Morrison
Ministering Evangelist
Cedar Crest Church of Christ
Dallas, TX

*   *   *

It is my pleasure to extend congratulations to my brother in Christ Carl Moore for taking on this project. Being a Black Deaf man, Carl lived in a world where the odds were stacked against him. Praise God that Carl did not succumb to society's expectations. This book reveals Carl's determination to rise above the odds. This struggle was not easy for Carl, but he leaned right into his discomfort and plowed forward with education, gainful employment, and community service—serving as mentor in the Black Deaf community. Carl further explains how he came to know the Lord Jesus Christ. The reader can see how none of his successes would have been accomplished without his ac6ve faith in God. Not only does Carl express his personal ab6ve faith in God: he also carefully outlines how others can come to know God through His Word. It is my hope that this book can educate and inspire the reader to self-examination.

Leonard Rufus, Co-Director
Cedar Crest Church of Christ Deaf Ministry Dallas, TX

*　　*　　*

PREFACE

FIRST OF ALL, I would like to thank all of you, my readers. My book is a true story of my life. I hope that my book will help you to understand about God, about His Son, Jesus Christ, about our world, and about my life. More so, what God expect (want) us to do with our lives.

INTRODUCTION

Let us, all people, focus on God and His book. Did you know what is the name of His book? We all should know that the name of His book is the Bible. And did you know what the Bible stands for? If you already know, that is great. If not, then please look what the Bible stands for:

B = Book or Bible

I = Instructs (Teaches)

B = Before

L = Leave

E = Earth

Obviously, that tells us something. It is telling us that God expects all of us to know Him without any excuses. In His book, God stated, 'I love those who love me, and those who look for me will find me. Proverbs 8:17 (ERV)

The wicked don't understand justice, but those who love the Lord understand it completely. Proverbs 28:5 (ERV)

Honestly, I cannot image whoever doesn't know God. So, for those people, who don't know God, I recommend that they read, "The Value of Wisdom," in the book of Proverbs 8:12–36 (ERV).

CHAPTER 1

Bible Reading

I. Bible Reading:

A. 1 John 5:1–5 (ERV)—God's Children Win Against the World

The people who believe that Jesus is the Christ are God's children. Anyone who loves the Father also loves the Father's children. How do we know that we love God's children? We know because we love God and we obey his commands. Loving God means obeying his commands. And God's commands are not too hard for us, because everyone who is a child of God has the power to win against the world. It is our faith that has won the victory against the world. So who wins against the world? Only those who believe that Jesus is the Son of God.

B. 1 John 5:18–21 (ERV)—We have Eternal Life Now

We know that those who have been made God's children do not continue to sin. The Son of God keeps them safe. The Evil One cannot hurt them. We know that we belong to God, but the Evil One controls the whole world. And we know that the Son of God has come and has given us understanding. So now we can know the one who is true, and we live in that true God. We are in his Son, Jesus Christ. He is the true God, and he is eternal life. So, dear children, keep yourselves away from false gods.

C. Genesis 1:1–31; 2; 1–3 (ERV)—The Beginning of the World

1. The First Day—Light—verses 1–5

God created the sky and the earth. At first, the earth was completely empty. There was nothing on the earth. Darkness covered the ocean, and God's Spirit moved over the water. Then God said, "Let there be light!" And light began to shine. He saw the light, and he knew that it was good. Then he separated the light from the darkness. God named the light "day," and he names the darkness "night." There was evening, and then there was morning. This was the first day.

2. The Second Day—Sky—verses 6–8

Then God said, "Let there be a space to separate the water into two parts!" So God made the space and separated the water. Some of the water was above it, and some of the water was below. God named that space "sky." There was evening, and then there was morning. This was the second day.

3. The Third Day—Dry Land and Plants—verses 9–13

Then God said, "Let the water under the sky be gathered together so that the dry land will appear." And it happened. God named the dry land "earth, and he named the water that was gathered together "sea." And God saw that this was good. Then God said, "Let the earth grow grass, plants that make grain, and fruit trees. The fruit trees will make fruit with seeds in it. And each plant will make its own kind of seed. Let these plants grow on the earth." And it happened. The earth grew grass and plants that made grain. And it grew trees that made fruit with seeds in it. Every plant made its own kind of seeds. And God saw that this was good. There was evening, and then there was morning. This was the third day.

4. The Fourth Day—Sun, Moon, and Stars—verses 14–19

Then God said, "Let there be lights in the sky. These lights will separate the days from the nights. They will be used for signs to show when special meetings begin and to the sky to shine light on the earth." And it happened. So God made the two large lights. He made the larger light to rule during the day and the smaller light to rule during the night. He also made the stars. God put these lights in the sky to shine on the earth. He put them in the sky to rule over the day and over the night. They separated the light from the darkness. And God saw that this was good. There was evening, and then there was morning. This was the fourth day.

5. The Fifth Day—Fish and Birds—verses 20–23

Then God said, "Let the water be filled with many living things, and let there be birds to fly in the air over the earth." So God created the large sea animals. He created all the many living things in the sea and every kind of bird that flies in the air. And God saw that this was good. God blessed all the living things in the sea and told them to have many babies and fill the seas. And he blessed the birds on land and told them to have many more babies. There was evening, and then there was morning. This was the fifth day.

6. The Sixth Day—Land Animals and People—verses 24–31

Then God said, "Let the earth produce many kinds of living things. Let there be many different kinds of animals. Let there be large animals and small crawling animals of every kind. And let all these animals produce more animals. And all these things happened. So God made every kind of animal. He made the wild animals, the tame animals, and all the small crawling things. And God saw that this was good. Then God said, "Now let's make humans who will be like us. They will rule over all the fish in the sea and the birds in the air. They will rule over all the large animals and all the little things that crawl on the earth." So God created humans in his own image. He created them to be like himself. He created them male and female. God blessed hem and said to them, "Have many children. Fill the earth and take control of it. Rule over the fish in the sea and the birds in the air. Rule over every living thing that moves on the earth." God said, "I am giving you all the grain bearing pants and all the fruit trees. These green plants will be their food. Every animal on earth, every bird in the air, and all the little things that crawl on the earth will eat that food." And all these things happened. God looked at everything he had made. And he saw that everything was very good. There was evening, and then there was morning. This was the sixth day.

7.   The Seventh Day—Rest—2:1–3

So the earth, the sky, and everything in them were finished. God finished the work he was doing, so on the seventh day he rested from his work. God blessed the seventh day and made it a holy day. He made it special because on that day he rested from all the work he did while creating the world.

D. Genesis 2:4–17 (ERV)—The Beginning of Humanity

This is the story about the creation of the sky and the earth. This is what happened when the Lord God made the earth and the sky. This was before there were plants on the earth. Nothing was growing in the fields because the Lord God had not yet made it rain on the earth, and there was no one to care for the plants. So water came up from the earth and spread over the ground. Then the Lord God took dust from the ground and made a man. He breathed the breath of life into the man's nose, and the man became a living thing. Then the Lord God planted a garden in the East, in a place named Eden. He put the man he made in that garden. Then the Lord God caused all the beautiful trees that were good for food to grow in the garden. In the middle of the garden, he put the tree of life and the tree that gives knowledge about the good and evil. A river flowed from Eden and watered the garden. The river then separated and became four smaller rivers. The name of the first river was Pishon. This river flowed around the entire country of Havilah. (There is gold in that country, and the gold is pure. A kind of expensive perfume and onyx are also found there.). The name of the second river was Gihon. The river flowed around the whole land of Cush. The name of the third river was Tigris. This river flowed east of Assyria. The fourth river was the Euphrates. The Lord God put the man in the Garden of Eden to work the soil and take care of the garden. The Lord God gave him this command: "You may eat from any tree in the garden. But you must not eat from the tree that gives knowledge about good and evil. If you eat fruit from that tree, on that day you will certainly die!

E. Genesis 2:18–25 (ERV)—A Companion for Adam

Then the Lord God said, "I see that it is not good for the man to be alone. I will make the companion he needs, one just right for him." The Lord God used dust from the ground and made every animal in the fields and every bird in the air. He brought all these animals to the man, and the man gave them all a name. The man gave names to all the tame animals, to all the birds in the air, and to all the wild animals. He saw many animals and birds, but he could not find a companion that was right for him. So the Lord God caused the man to sleep very deeply. While he was asleep, God took on of the ribs from the man's body. The he closed the man's skin where the rib had been. The Lord God used the rib from the man to make a woman. Then he brought the woman to the man. And the man said, "Finally! One like me, with bones from my bones and a body from my body. She was taken out of a man so I will call her woman." That is why a man leaves his father and mother and is joined to his wife. In this way two people become one. The man and his wife were naked, but they were not ashamed.

F.   Genesis 3:1–24 (ERV)—The Beginning of Sin

The snake was the most clever of all the wild animals that the Lord God had made. The snake spoke to the woman and said, "Woman, did God really tell you that you must not eat from any tree in the garden?" The woman answered the snake, "No, we can eat fruit from the trees in the garden. But there is one tree we must not eat from. God told us, 'You must not eat fruit from the tree that is in the middle of the garden. You must not even touch that tree, or you will die.'" But the snake said to the woman, "You will not die. God knows that if you eat the fruit from that tree you will learn abut good and evil, and then you will be like God!" The woman could see that the tree was beautiful and the fruit looked so good to eat. She also liked the idea that it would make her wise. So she took some of the fruit from the tree and ate it. Her husband was there with her, so she gave him some of the fruit, and he ate it. Then it was as if their eyes opened, and they saw things differently. They saw that they were naked. So they got some fig leaves, sewed them together, and wore them for clothes. During the cool part of the day, the Lord God was walking in the garden. The man and the woman heard him, and they hid among the trees in the garden. The Lord God called to the man and said, "Where are you?" The man said, "I heard you walking in the garden, and I was afraid.

I was naked, so I hid." The Lord God said to the man, "Who told you that you were naked? Did you eat fruit from that special tree? I told you not to eat from that tree!" The man said, "The woman you put here with me gave me fruit from that tree. So I ate it." Then the Lord God said to the woman, "What have you done?" She said, "The snake tricked me, so I ate the fruit." So the Lord God said to the snake, "You did this very bad thing, so bad things will happen to you. It will be worse for you than for any other animal. You must crawl on your belly and eat dust all the days of your life. I will make you and the woman enemies to each other. Your children and her children will be enemies. You will bite her child's foot, but he will crush your head." Then the Lord God said to the woman, "I will cause you to have much trouble when you are pregnant. And when you give birth to children, you will have much pain. You will want your husband very much, but he will rule over you." Then the Lord God said to the man, "I commanded you not to eat from that tree. But you listened to your wife and ate from it. So I will curse the ground because of you. You will have to work hard all your life for the food the ground produces. The ground will grow Thors and weeds for you. And you will have to eat the plants that grow wild in the fields. You will work hard for your food, until your face is covered with sweat. You will work hard until the day you die, and then you will become dust again. I used dust to make you, and when you die, you will become dust again. Adam named his wife Eve. He gave her this name because Eve would be the mother of everyone who ever lived. The Lord God used animal skins and made some clothes for the man and his wife. Then he put the clothes on them. The Lord God said, "Look, the man has become like us—he knows about good and evil. And now the man might take the fruit from the tree of life. If the magnets that fruit, he will live forever." So the Lord God forced the man out of the Garden of Eden to work the ground he was made from. Then he put Cherub angels and a sword of fire at the entrance to the garden to protect it. The sword flashed around and around, guarding the way to the tree of life.

G. Galatians 5:19–26 (ERV)—The Spirit and Human Nature (Two Kinds of People in this world)

The wrong things the sinful self does are clear: committing sexual sin, being morally bad, doing all kinds of shameful things, worshiping false gods, taking part in witchcraft, hating people, causing trouble, being jealous, angry or selfish, causing people to argue and divide into separate groups, being filled with envy, getting drunk, having wild parties, and doing other things like this. I warn you now as I warned you before: The people who do these things will not have a part in God's kingdom. But the fruit that the Spirit produces in a person's life is love, joy, peace, patience, kindness, goodness, faithfulness, gentleness, and self-control. There is no law against these kinds of things. Those who belong to Christ Jesus have crucified their sinful self. They have given up their old selfish feelings and the evil things they wanted to do. We get our new life from the Spirit, so we should follow the Spirit. We must not feel proud and boast about ourselves. We must not cause trouble for each other or be jealous of each other.

H. Philippians 2:12–18 (ERV)—Be the People God Wants You to Be

My dear friends, you always obeyed what you were taught. Just as you obeyed when I was with you, it is even more important for you to obey now that I am not there. So you must continue to live in a way that gives meaning to your salvation. Do this with fear and respect for God. Yes, it is God who is working in you. He helps you want to do what pleases him, and he gives you the power to do it. Do everything without complaining or arguing so that you will be blameless and pure, children of God without any fault. But you are living with evil people all round you, who have lost their sense of what is right. Among those people you shine like lights in a dark world, and you offer them the teaching that gives life. So I can be proud of you when Christ comes again. You will show that my work was not wasted—that I ran in the race and won. Your faith makes you give your lives as a sacrifice in serving God. Maybe I will have to offer my own life with your sacrifice. But if that happens, I will be glad, and I will share my joy with all of you. You also should be glad and share your joy with me.

I. Colossians 2:6–7 (ERV)—Continue to Live in Christ

You accepted Christ Jesus as Lord, so continue to live following him. You must depend on Christ only, drawing life and strength from him. Just as you were taught the truth, continue to grow stronger in your understanding of it. And never stop giving thanks to God.

J. Mark 16:15–16 (ERV)—Jesus Talks to His Followers

He said to them, "Go everywhere in the world. Tell the Good News to everyone. Whoever believes and is baptized will be saved. But those who do not believe will be judged guilty."

K. 1 Peter 3:15 (ERV)—Suffering for Doing Right

But keep the Lord Christ holy in your hearts. Always be ready to answer everyone who asks you to explain about the hope you have.

L. Psalm 62:5 (ERV)—A song of David

I must calm down and turn to God; he is my only hope.

M. Acts 4:20 (ERV)—Must tell people

We cannot be quiet. We must tell people about what we have seen and heard.

N. John 15:18 (ERV)—Jesus Warns His Followers

If the world hates you, remember that they hated me first.

O. Philippians 4:13 (ERV)—Paul Thanks the Philippian Believers

Christ is the one who gives me the strength I need to do whatever I must do.

CHAPTER 2

Who Is God?

GOD IS OUR Creator and Ruler of the universe. He is the most extreme superhero. He can do anything and everything. He is also our heavenly Father. He knows all our weaknesses, thoughts, and words. He knows our actions and our needs. He is so great the he is everywhere at the same time. He is more powerful than anything else. He is forgiving, wise, and truthful. He loves us so much that he sent His Son, Jesus, to earth to save us from our sins. He promised that if we believe in His Son, Jesus, our souls will live forever with Him. You can know God by having faith in His Son, Jesus, and by doing what God wants you to do. The Bible tells us all about God and what we need to do to please Him.

Isiah 40:28

Isaiah 40:18

Jeremiah 32:17

Matthew 6:9

Psalm 103:14

Psalm 44:21

Psalm 103:14

Matthew 6:32

Jeremiah 23:23–24

Revelation 19:6

Psalm 136

Colossians 2:2–3

Titus 1:2

John 3:16

John 14:1, 6

Mark 3:35

CHAPTER 3

What Were the Problems in this World?

I WOULD SAY that we should know that in our today's world is full of:

1. Suffering—Great pain, sickness, or sadness. Suffering is when you feel really bad. It might be because you are sick or hurt. Or it might be because someone has hurt your feelings. Jesus suffered. After He was arrested, the people did things to embarrass Him. His disciples weren't there for Him. All of this hurt His feelings. Jesus also suffered great pain when He was crucified on the cross. His followers suffered for telling the truth about Him. Some suffered in prisons. Others suffered as they died for believing in Him.

Matthew 27:27–31
John 18:1–5, 15–18, 25–27
Mark 15:22–37

2. Disease—an illness that affects a person, animal, or plant, with specific symptoms;

3. Accident—a situation in which someone is hurt or something is damaged without anyone intending it to happen;

4. Corruption—dishonest or immoral behavior;

5. Hate—The opposite of love. If you hate something, you don't like anything about it. Jesus taught that we shouldn't hate our enemies. Instead, we should love them. But there are some things that God hates—and we should, too. He hates "proud eyes, a lying tongue, and hands that kill those who aren't guilty. He also hates heart that make evil plans, feet that are quick to do evil, any witness who pours out lies, and anyone who stirs up family fights."

Luke 6:27

Proverbs 6:16–19

6. Bitterness—angry and upset because you feel something bad or unfair has happened to you;

7. Immorality—morally wrong, and not accepted by society; living or continuing forever;

8. Destroyed families—to damage something so badly that it cannot be used or no longer exists;

9. Wickedness—Evil or sinful things. Wicked people do bad things on purpose! The Bible says, "The Lord protects everyone who follows Him, but the wicked follow a road that leads to run." The book of Job explains how God treats the wicked. They might be rich and wear fancy clothes, but their nice things will be taken from them and given to God's people. "Those sinners may go to bed rich, but they will wake up poor." Does wickedness scare you?

Don't worry! Job also says, "God rescues the needy from the words of the wicked and the fist of the mighty."

Psalm 1:6

Job 2:13–19

Job 5:15

10. Drug—an illegal substance that people smoke, inject, etc. for pleasure;

11. Drunkenness—Drinking too much alcohol. Not only is drinking bad for your health, but it can get you into a lot of trouble. The Bible warns about drunkenness. It can lead people to sin. Instead of filling up on alcohol, people should fill up on the Spirit of God.

Proverbs 23:21

Ephesians 5:18

12. Envy—the feeling of wanting to have the qualities or things that someone else has;

13. Murder—Taking the life of another human being. It is wrong to kill. One of the Ten Commandments says, "Do not murder."

Exodus 20:13

14. War—a time when two or more countries, or opposing groups within a county, fight each other with soldiers and weapons;

15. Arguments—a disagree meant, especially one in which people are angry and shout;

16. Backbiting—Saying bad things about others behind their backs. The Bible says that backbiting is not good behavior for anyone, especially Christians.

Romans 1:30

Proverbs 25:23

17. Backsliding—Knowing God, then turning away from Him. Backsliding is bad because it keeps us away from God. Some people backslide because they don't grow in their faith. Others backslide when they lose their faith in bad times. Sometimes people love the things they own more than they love God. That causes backsliding, too.

Isaiah 59:2

18. Pride—Being conceited (clever or intelligent). A little pride is a good thing. When you work hard and are pleased with your work, it's fine to be proud. But a lot of pride will get you in trouble. If you go around talking about how great you are, people will notice. And they probably won't like what they see. A good example of foolish pride is in Luke 18:11–12: "The Pharisee stood up and prayed about himself: 'God, I thank you that I am not like other men—robbers, evildoers, adulterers—or even like this tax collector. I fast twice a week and give a tenth of all I get'" (NIV). In other words, he stood up and said, "Hey God, look how great I am. You made me better than everybody else." That's foolish pride.

Proverbs 16:18

19. Revenge—Getting even. Have you ever wanted to do something to get back at a person who harmed you? No one likes to be hurt, but we must remember that revenge is wrong. Jesus said, "But I tell you not to try to get even with a person who has done something to you." He said we must love our enemies as well as our neighbors. We should pray for anyone who mistreats us.

Matthew 5:39

Matthew 5:43–44

20. Arrogance—behaving in a rude way because you think you are more important than other people;

21. Hunger—a person or animal that hunts wild animals; someone who is looking for a particular thing;

22. Homelessness—people who do not have a place to live, and who often live in the streets; without a home;

23. Pain—the feeling you have when part of your body hurts;

24. Hurt—to injure yourself or someone else;

25. Selfishness—caring only about yourself and not about other people;

26. Greed—Wanting a lot more stuff. When your mind is set on getting a bunch of stuff, Satan will work on you. He will try to get you to put your faith in things instead of God. Jesus warned against greed. He said a good Christian life is not built on things. It is built on setting your mind on God.

1 Timothy 6:7–10

27. Death—The end of our physical lives. Everyone is born and dies. Nothing can change that. But, when our bodies die, it doesn't mean the end of life. God promises life forever with Him if we believe in Jesus Christ. Although

your body dies, your soul—the person you are in your heart—will live on with God. People who don't believe in Jesus face something called the "second death." It means that their sounds don't go with God. They are separated from Him forever.

John 3:16

Revelation 21:8

28. Cheat—to behave in a dishonest way in order to win or get an advantage;

CHAPTER 4

What Did God Do?

God did three things to save our world:

1. It was His will to send His Son, Jesus Christ, so that we all could live.
2. It was His will to send His Son, Jesus Christ, to be the satisfaction (died) for our sins.
3. It was His will to send His Son, Jesus Christ, to be the Savior of the world.

John 16:33

CHAPTER 5

What Does God Expect (Want) From Us?

In other word, what we must do? First, we must believe that Jesus is the Christ born of God. 1 John 5:1 We must also believe in the incarnation (or "the coming in the flesh") of Jesus. We must read, study, and learn more about God and His word. We must show our love by keeping God's commandments. The commandments are list of our obligations, the assignments that we have one toward another. We are to minister (to give aid or service) to one another, admonish (to criticize or warn gently but seriously; to give friendly advice or encouragement) one another, exhort one another, and serve one another. Commandment keeping, then, is a demonstration of our love for the Father of our love for His children. We must all meet all of the assignments that God has given us regarding worship, concerning prayer, concerning walking in the light, concerning believing His Son, and meeting all of the obligations that God has given to us. Pleasing God would be one of the major interests and commitments on the part of God's people.

Philippians 2:12–18 (ERV)—Be the People God Wants You to Be

My dear friends, you always obeyed what you were taught. Just as you obeyed when I was with you, it is even more important for you to obey now that I am not there. So you must continue to live in a way that gives meaning to your salvation. Do this with fear and respect for God. Yes, it is God who is working in you. He helps you want to do what pleases him, and he gives you the power to do it. Do everything without complaining or arguing so that you will be blameless and pure, children of God without any fault. But you are living with evil people all round you, who have lost their sense of what is right. Among those people you shine like lights in a dark world, and you offer them the teaching that gives life. So I can be proud of you when Christ comes again. You will show that my work was not wasted—that I ran in the race and won. Your faith makes you give your lives as a sacrifice in serving God. Maybe I will have to offer my own life with your sacrifice. But if that happens, I will be glad, and I will share my joy with all of you. You also should be glad and share your joy with me.

Colossians 2:6–7 (ERV)—Continue to Live in Christ

You accepted Christ Jesus as Lord, so continue to live following him. You must depend on Christ only, drawing life and strength from him. Just as you were taught the truth, continue to grow stronger in your understanding of it. And never stop giving thanks to God.

1 John 5:18–21 (ERV)—We have Eternal Life Now

We know that those who have been made God's children do not continue to sin. The Son of God keeps them safe. The Evil One cannot hurt them. We know that we belong to God, but the Evil One controls the whole world. And we know that the Son of God has come and has given us understanding. So now we can know the one who is true, and we live in that true God. We are in his Son, Jesus Christ. He is the true God, and he is eternal life. So, dear children, keep yourselves away from false gods.

CHAPTER 6

What Was Carl's Life Like?

CARL SELECTED THIS newspaper article from the DEMOCRAT AND CHRONICLE, ROCHESTER, NY, TUESDAY, FEBRUARY 11, 1992, called, "SPEAKING OUT, Life's a struggle when you're BLACK and DEAF, by Carl Moore." In this article, it stated, "As we celebrate national Black History Month, cities throughout the country are sponsoring exhibits, theater presentation, workshops, panel discussing, and lectures that celebrate the rich cultural heritage of black Americans. These activities serve not only to instill pride and educate, but also to draw much needed attention to the plight of black people today.

Some might scoff at the use of the word "plight," but these statistics show why that word is frighteningly appropriate:

- Twenty-five percent of black males between the ages of 20–29 are in prison, on parole, or on probation. Their numbers far exceed the number of black males who attend college.
- The National Research Council said in 1989 that economic gains made by black people since 1940 had stopped.
- Homicide is the leading cause of death for 15-20-year-old black males.

Those statistics worsen when a new dimension is added—the dimension of deafness. A 1979 report showed that the unemployment rate among black deaf males is five times greater than that of deaf white males, who themselves traditionally face higher unemployment and earn lower salaries than their hearing peers. Truly, to be a black deaf male in today's society presents challenges. Some would find them overwhelming. As a youngstar growing up in Philadelphia, I did.

I attended regular public schools. I grew up struggling to master both the "black English," spoken by the black community and English as spoken by the white community. I was the only black deaf person at my high school who spoke, rather than used sign language (there were three oral white students). I had very little exposure to the deaf community, and even less to the black deaf community.

I planned early on to get myself to college and I did. I graduated from the National Technical Institute for the Deaf, a college of Rochester Institute of Technology, in 1974 and, 14 years later. I returned to Rochester to accept a counseling job at my alma mater.

I QUICKLY found myself in the role of informal adviser to a small group of black deaf male students. These students, I found, needed more than advice about which class to take. I became mentor, teacher, father, brother, friend and counselor. We discussed everything from personal difficulties to academic problems.

For the past four years the expectations of my student friends have grown, and so have my own expectations, both for myself and for the black deaf community in general. A pressing need exists to make things better for young black deaf men today. Here are some suggesting:

- Increase the number of young men attending and graduating from college.
- Encourage more black deaf men working in schools to serve as role models for students.

- Increase the number of organizations nationwide that can stimulate and help young deaf black men by offering them leadership and advocacy roles.
- Conduct more research about the employment and unemployment rates of black deaf men.
- Encourage black deaf men to write and publish articles about their experiences in professional journals.
- Develop mentoring networks among black deaf men.

This list indeed is weighty. I've asked myself difference can one person make. One step that I've taken is most recently, to become president of the National Black Deaf Advocates organization. As president, my personal challenge is to bring together black deaf people and supporters to further the needs and aspirations of black people who are deaf.

A national conference will be held this March in Atlanta. Its theme, "Excellence and Equity," describe the conference's goals. Throughout the three-day conference, role models who generate, nurture, and aim for excellence and equality in the context of personal, community, and educational environments will inspire us.

As individuals and by working together we can bring about change. The future of thousands of black deaf men and women depends on us.

Moore, the president of the National Black Deaf Advocates, is a career development counselor at the National Technical Institute for the Deaf, a college of Rochester Institute of Technology.

CHAPTER 7

How Did Carl Finally Become A Minister?

DURING THE YEAR of 1999 or 2000, when I visited at the Virginia Association of the Deaf (VAD), that was when I first met Minister Mark Lowenstein. He is deaf, and he invited me to come and visit his church at Fairfax Church of Christ (FXCC) Deaf Ministry in Fairfax County, Virginia. I believed that it was the next day on Sunday when my wife, Nina, and I went and visited his church. Honestly, we, Nina and I, were impressed, because Mark used his power point slides along with his professional sign language/voice interpreter. Also, at the same time, Mark used American Sign Language (ASL) while he taught his Sunday school Bible class, then he preached at his worship service. Somehow, we, Nina and I, began to visit his church often. Then, eventually, we joined his church. After few years, I asked Mark, "Where did you go to college in order to become a minister?" As soon as I received information from Mark where he went for training, I applied there at Sunset International Bible Institutes (SIBI) in 2004. Then I was accepted. Then Nina and I moved to Lubbock, TX around July 2004 until I graduated in May 2007. Then I became an Intern at the Park

Plaza Church of Christ (PPCC) Deaf Ministry as Minister/Counselor for the Deaf in Tulsa, Oklahoma during the summer of 2007 for about 8 weeks. After that, PPCC offered me a part-time job from May 2008 to May 2010. Then I stayed and worked at PPCC for full-time job from May 2010 until I retired on December 31, 2018. Then Nina and I moved to Dallas, TX, where I became a part-time Co-Director of the Cedar Crest Church of Christ (CCCC) Deaf Ministry with Brother Leonard Rufus from February 4, 2019 to present time.

CHAPTER 8

Be Right With God

WE HAVE BEEN made right with God because of our faith. So we have peace with God through our Lord Jesus Christ. Through our faith, Christ has brought us into that blessing of God's grace that we now enjoy. And we are very happy because of the hope we have of sharing God's glory. And we are also happy with the troubles we have. Why are we happy with troubles? Because we know that these troubles make us more patient. And this patience is proof that we are strong. And this proof gives us hope. And this hope will never disappoint us. We know this because God has poured out his love to fill our hearts through the Holy Spirit he gave us. Christ died for us when we were unable to help ourselves. We were living against God, but at just the right time Christ died for us. Very few people will die to save the life of someone else, even if it is for a good person. Someone might be willing to die for an especially good person. But Christ died for us while we were still sinners, and by this God showed how much he loves us. We have been made right with God by the blood sacrifice of Christ. So through Christ we will surely be saved from God's anger. I mean that while we were God's enemies, he made friends with us through his Son's death. And the fact that we are now God's friends makes it even more certain that he will save us through his

Son's life. And not only will we be saved, but we also rejoice right now in what God has done for us through our Lord Jesus Christ. It is because of Jesus that we are now God's friends.

Romans 5:1–11 (ERV)

Believe it or not, even though I have been fighting all my life. Even today, I am still fighting against this world. While I was growing up with my family in the Black Community, I fought a lot within my family, with my relatives, with my neighbors, and with my enemies. But God taught me that these battles were not mine. That means that the Lord God tells us, "No more fighting." And because I belong to the Lord Jesus Christ, He told me that I must settle with my disagreement. So, I learned that Christ is more important than anything in this world. So, again, I must do what is right. I can talk it out instead of fight. Why is that happened? Honestly, I do not like to talk more about it, because it was all in the past. Even, today, I must often pray and ask God for help and forgive me again, again and again.

Philippians 3:1–11

CHAPTER 9

Prayer

(See also Faith; Forgiveness)

PRAYER MEANS THAT you communicate with God. It also means that you can pray to God anytime. You don't have to wait in line. God is so powerful that He can talk—and listen—to everyone at once. There are lots of reasons to pray. You can ask God to help you and others. You can ask Him for things you need. You can tell God that you're sorry for the bad things you've done. You can even pray to Him when you need someone to talk to. When you pray, you should always remember to thank God and tell Him how great He is. When you are done talking, take some time to listen to what He has to say.

Ephesians 6:18

Luke 11:3

1 John 1:9

Jesus also teaches us about prayer.—Matthew 6:5–15 (ERV)

When you pray, don't be like the hypocrites. They love to stand in the synagogues and on the street corners and pray loudly. They want people to see them. The truth is, that's all the reward they will get. But when you pray, you should go into your room and close the door. Then pray to your Father. He is there in that private place. He can see what is done in private, and he will reward you. And when you pray, don't be like the people who don't know God. They say the same things again and again. They think that if they say it enough, their god will hear them. Don't be like them. Your Father knows what you need before you ask him. So this is how you should pray:

'Our Father in heaven,
    we pray that your name will always be
        kept holy.
We pray that your kingdom will come—
    that what you want will be done here
        on earth, the same as in heaven.
Give us the food we need for each day.
Forgive our sins,
    just as we have forgiven those who did
        wrong to us.
Don't let us be tempted,
    but save us from the Evil One.'

Yes, if you forgive others for the wrongs they do to you, then your Father in heaven will also forgive your wrongs. Bt if you don't forgive others, then your Father in heaven will not forgive the wrongs you do.

CHAPTER 10

Carl's Favorite 2 Songs

HE NEVER HAS LEFT ME ALONE

Since I gave to Jesus my poor broken heart
He never has let me alone
Since my goal to heaven eternal did start

(Chorus)   He never has left me alone
He never has left me alone
By night and by day
Jesus is with me always
He never has left me alone

The time may be rough, rocky, and long
He never has left me alone
The day may be dismal, the nights may be long
He never has left me alone

(Chorus)   He never has left me alone
He never has left me alone
By night and by day
Jesus is with me always
He never has left me alone

When the sorrows take by heart by surprise

He never has left me alone

In tenderness He wipes the tears from my eyes

He never has left me alone

(Chorus)   He never has left me alone
He never has left me alone
By night and by day
Jesus is with me always
He never has left me alone

IT IS A GOOD DAY TO LOVE JESUS

It is a good day to Love Jesus. (Sing it 3 times)

Walk! Walk! Walk! (Sing it 3 times)

In the light of God.

It is a good day to Serve Jesus. (Sing it 3 times)

Walk! Walk! Walk! (Sing it 3 times)

In the light of God.

It is a good day to Praise Jesus. (Sing it 3 times)

Walk! Walk! Walk! (Sing it 3 times)

In the light of God.

It is a good day to Follow Jesus. (Sing it 3 times)

Walk! Walk! Walk! (Sing it 3 times)

In the light of God.

It is a good day to Obey Jesus. (Sing it 3 times)

Walk! Walk! Walk! (Sing it 3 times)

In the light of God.

It is a good day to Honor Jesus. (Sing it 3 times)

Walk! Walk! Walk! (Sing it 3 times)

In the light of God.

CONCLUSION

IT IS ONLY one thing that man needs is victory over the world. How? Have faith in Jesus Christ. How? By believing that Jesus Christ is the Son of God. Also, remember what the Bible said, especially to this who have a little faith in Him: Jesus told His followers, "Go everywhere in the world. Tell the Good News to everyone. Whoever believes and is baptized will be saved. But those who do not believe will be judged guilty.

Mark 16:15–16 (ERV)

ABOUT THE AUTHOR/WRITER/
TEACHER/COUNSELOR

CARL WAS BORN and raised in Philadelphia, PA to a deceased hearing father and deceased deaf mother. He is the second oldest of seven children (three hearing and four deaf). Carl and his wife, Nina, were married in 1998 and have four grown children. Although Carl is originally from Philadelphia, PA, he has lived many places.

He is a graduate of: National Technical Institute for the Deaf/Rochester Institute of Technology (NTID/RIT) with AAS degree in Business Technology ('74),

Gallaudet University (GU) with BA degree in Social Work ('81), New York University (NYU) with MA degree in Deafness Rehabilitation ('83). He also holds a Certificate of Ordination and Certification in Biblical and Deaf Ministry Studies in May 2007 and a BA degree in Biblical and Deaf Ministry Studies in May 2009.

Carl's experiences include a number of minister/counselor internships at congregations from Florida to Oklahoma, even working eight summers with a Deaf Foreign Mission Team in Kenya, Africa, between 2006 and 2017. More so, Carl has published two books called, "God Answered Me in Tough Times: My First Deaf Missionary Trip to Kenya, Africa in 2006." Carl's third book called, "Brotherly Love," came in around the Fall of 2021. Recently, he just published his fourth book called, "Taking the World by Storm." You can purchase these books through his link: authorcarlm-moore.com.

Carl was employed as Minister/Counselor for the Deaf/Hard of Hearing at Park Plaza Church of Christ (PPCC) Deaf Ministry in Tulsa, OK, from June 1, 2008 until he retired on December 31, 2018. Then he moved to Dallas, TX on January 26, 2019. Then he became Co-Director of Deaf Ministry on February 4, 2019 at Cedar Crest Church of Christ (CCCC) in Dallas, TX. He continued to have a great desire to reach out to the lost deaf people, hard of hearing people, and those who associate with them by sharing the Gospel of Jesus with them.

www.ingramcontent.com/pod-product-compliance
Lightning Source LLC
Chambersburg PA
CBHW041126120626

46547CB00019B/2870